Pick Me

#3 - in the Wallflowers Series
50 drawings by Joan Worth

©2018 Joan Worth
ALL RIGHTS RESERVED
De Pere, Wisconsin
ISBN 13: 978-1983733109
ISBN-10: 1983733105

Pick Me #3 Wallflowers Series - ©2018 Joan Worth

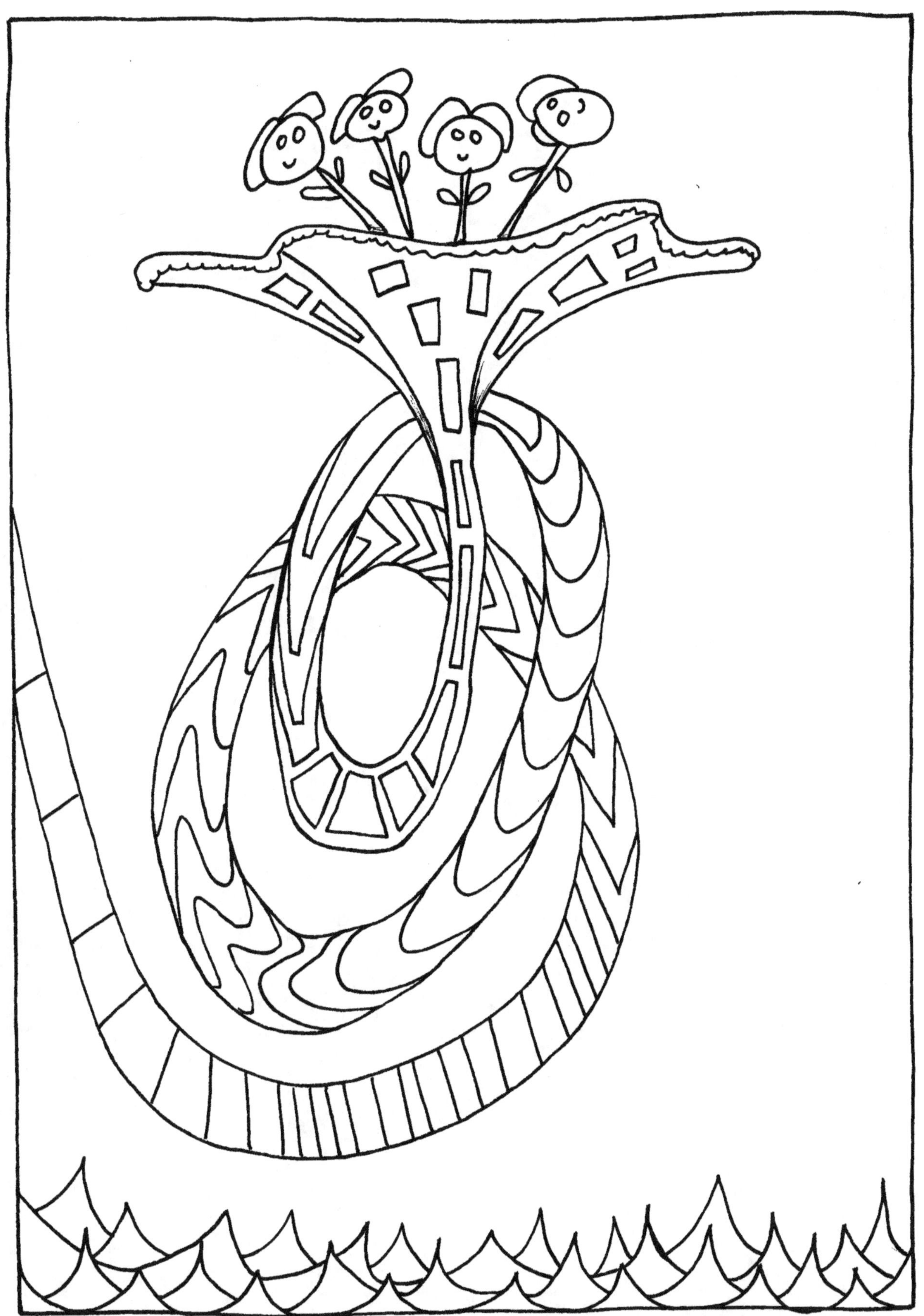

Pick Me #3 Wallflowers Series - ©2018 Joan Worth

Pick Me #3 Wallflowers Series - ©2018 Joan Worth

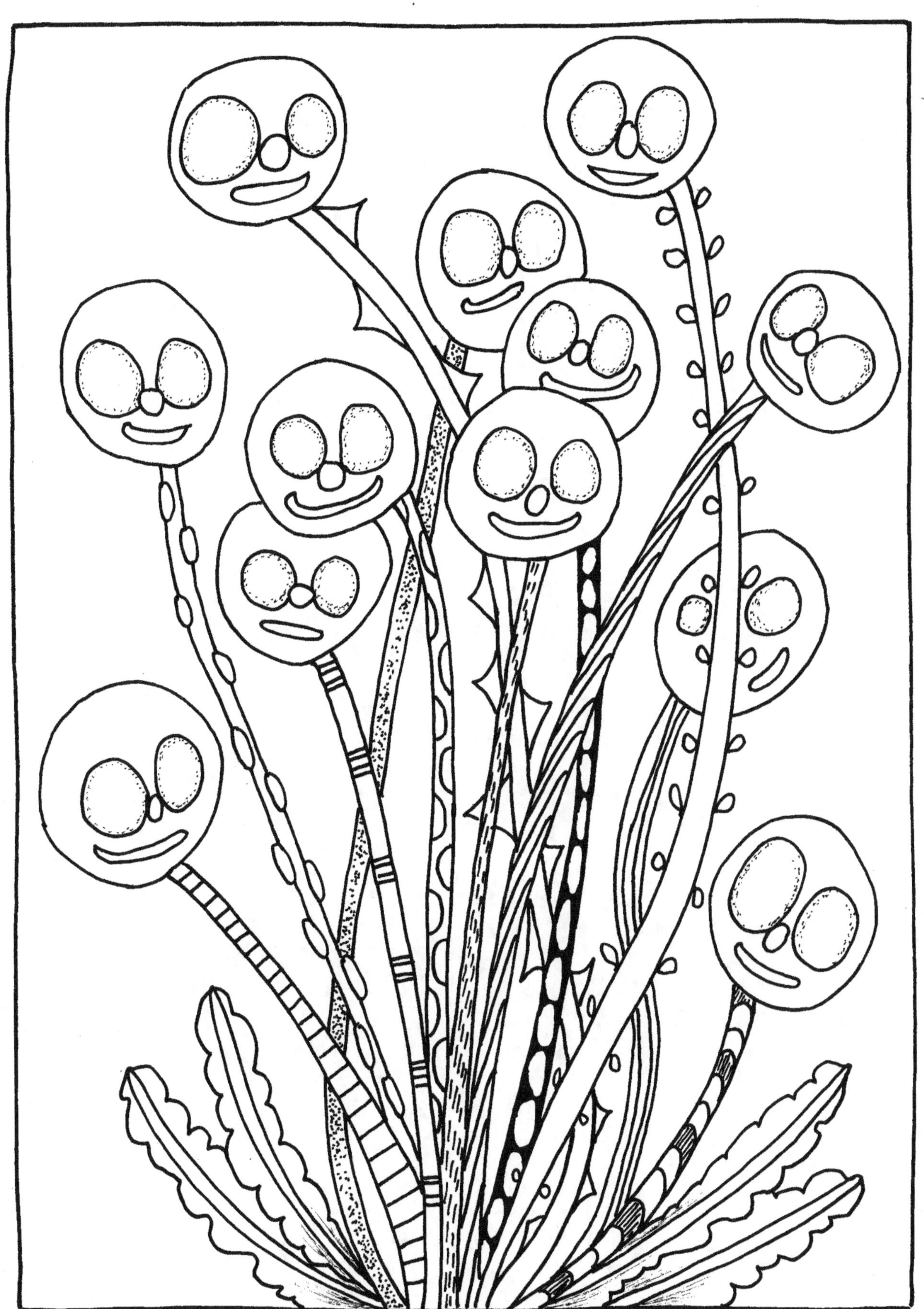

Pick Me #3 Wallflowers Series - ©2018 Joan Worth

Pick Me #3 Wallflowers Series - ©2018 Joan Worth

Pick Me #3 Wallflowers Series - ©2018 Joan Worth

Pick Me #3 Wallflowers Series - ©2018 Joan Worth

Pick Me #3 Wallflowers Series - ©2018 Joan Worth

Pick Me #3 Wallflowers Series - ©2018 Joan Worth

Pick Me #3 Wallflowers Series - ©2018 Joan Worth

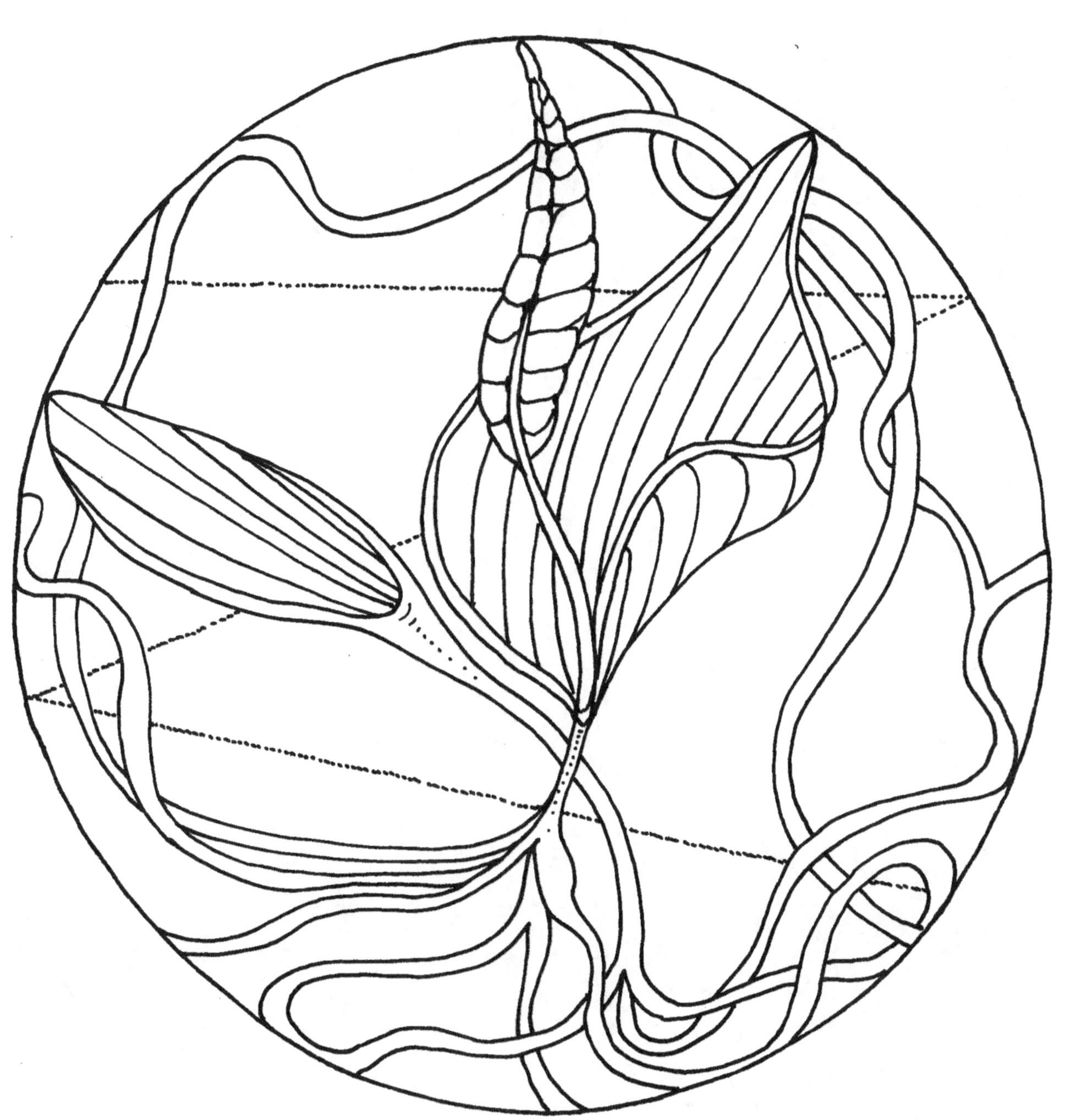

Pick Me #3 Wallflowers Series - ©2018 Joan Worth

Pick Me #3 Wallflowers Series - ©2018 Joan Worth

Pick Me #3 Wallflowers Series - ©2018 Joan Worth

Pick Me #3 Wallflowers Series - ©2018 Joan Worth

Pick Me #3 Wallflowers Series - ©2018 Joan Worth

Pick Me #3 Wallflowers Series - ©2018 Joan Worth

Pick Me #3 Wallflowers Series - ©2018 Joan Worth

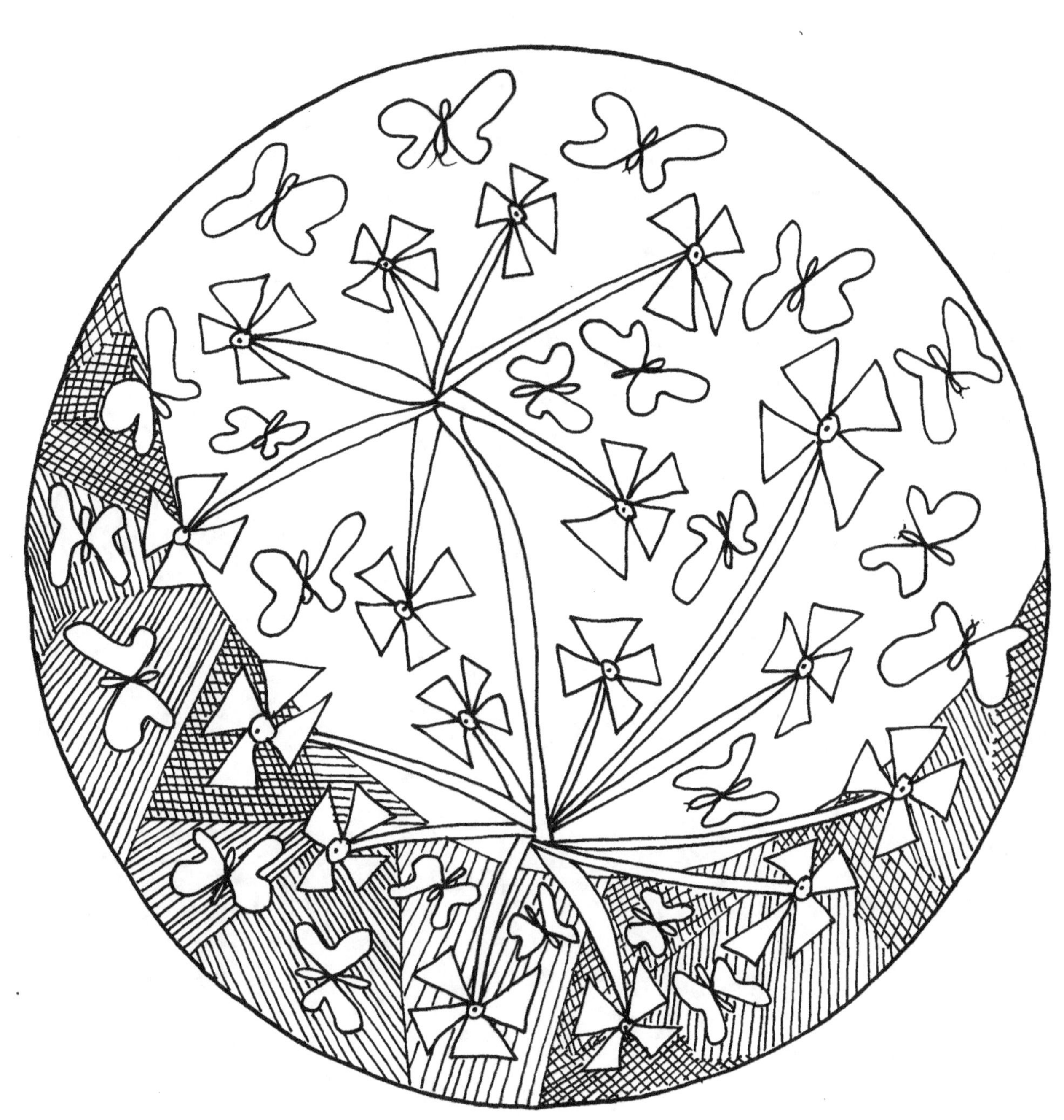

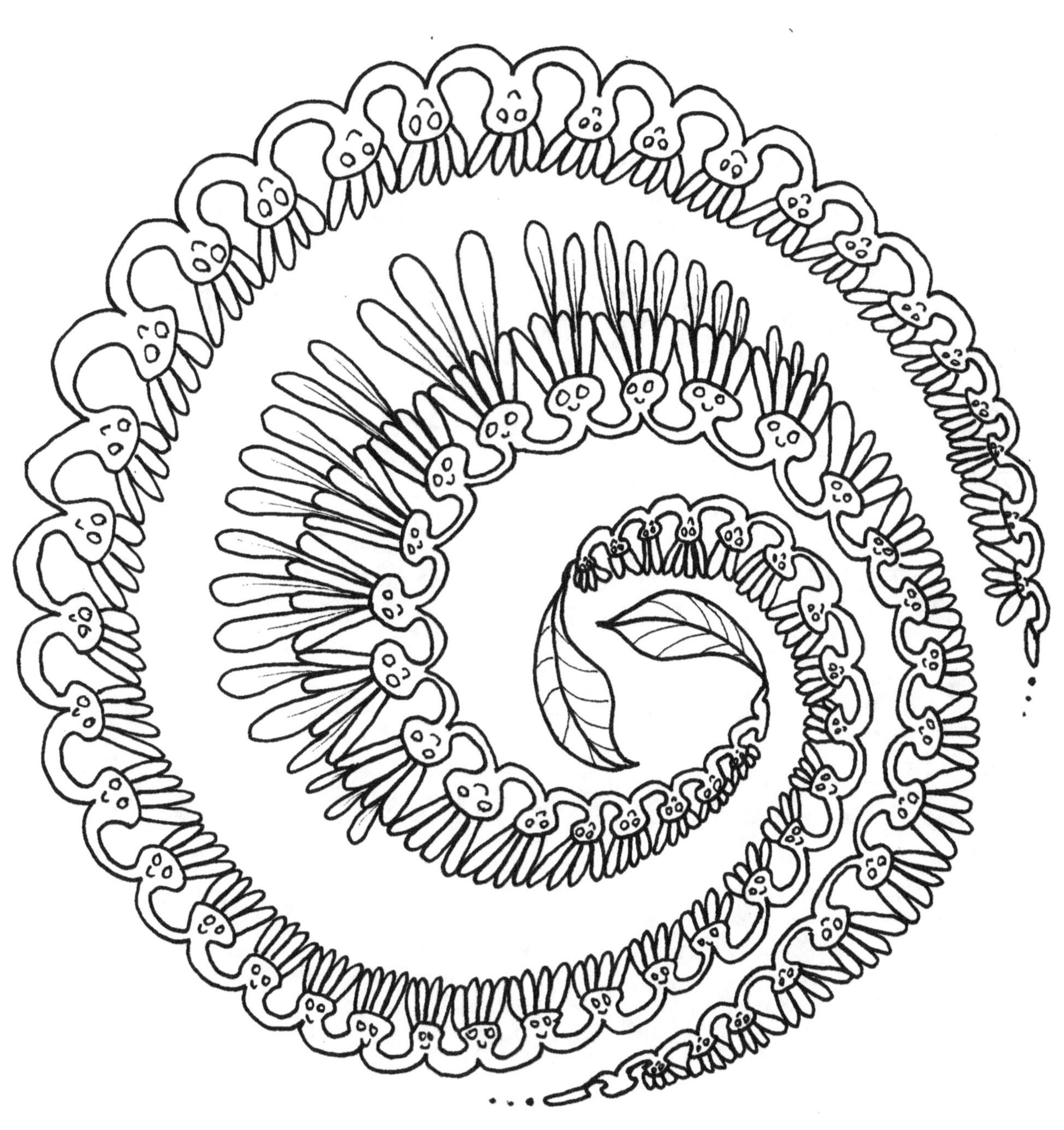

www.ingramcontent.com/pod-product-compliance
Lightning Source LLC
Chambersburg PA
CBHW081312250726
48662CB00008B/2522